INSECTS

Theresa Greenaway

Emperor moth

A Golden Photo Guide from St. Martin's Press

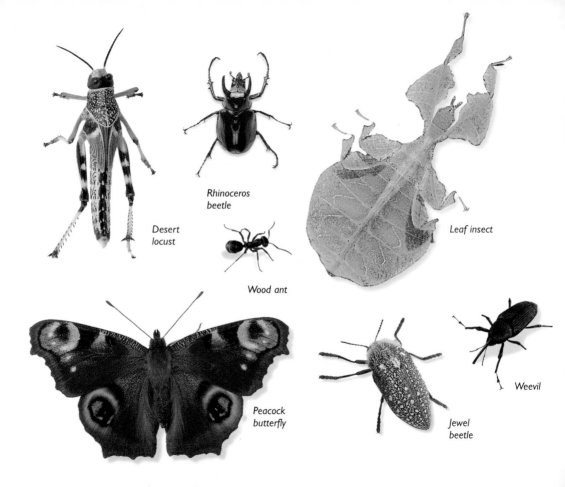

Desert
locust

Rhinoceros
beetle

Wood ant

Leaf insect

Peacock
butterfly

Jewel
beetle

Weevil

INSECTS

A Golden Photo Guide from St. Martin's Press

Harlequin bugs

St. Martin's Press

New York

Manufactured in China

Produced by
Elm Grove Books Limited

Series Editor Susie Elwes
Art Director Susi Martin
Illustration John Woodcock
Index Hilary Bird

Original Edition © 2000
Image Quest Limited
This edition © 2001
Elm Grove Books Limited

St. Martin's Press
175 Fifth Avenue
New York
N.Y.10010.
www.stmartins.com

A CIP catalogue record for this
book is available from the
Library of Congress

ISBN 1-58238-176-3

Text and Photographs in this
book previously published in
Eyewitness 3D Insects

This edition published 2001

ACKNOWLEDGMENTS
Bob Brock: 36; **Jane Burton**: 27, 36, 44, 46; NHPA 16, 19, 30, 34, 41, 44, 45, 48, 48;
Tim Hellier: 13, 15, 18, 22, 25, 26, 2, 28, 29, 32, 33, 37, 39, 42, 49, 51; **Chris Parks**:Title,
4 5, 10,11, 21, 23, 29, 31, 34, 41, 51;**Peter Parks**: 6, 8, 9, 12, 13, 14, 17, 19, 26, 30, 31, 35,
38, 39, 40, 41, 43, 45, 48, 49, 50, 51, 53; **Justin Peach**: 7, 14, 15, 16, 18, 20, 21, 22, 27, 39,
47, 53; **Kim Taylor**: Titles, 5, 6, 11, 13, 17, 18, 24, 24, 24, 25, 25, 26, 32, 33, 33, 37, 37, 38,
40, 42, 46, 46, 47, 47, 52, 52, 54, 55, 56, 56, 58, 59, Index

Privet hawk moth

CONTENTS

Fly

WHAT IS AN INSECT?

FLY WINGS
Flies, such as this greenbottle, only have one pair of wings. Instead of hind wings, they have a pair of tiny, knobbed balancing organs, called halteres.

Hoverfly

So many new insects are constantly being discovered that no one knows how many kinds there are. There may be at least five million different species! Insects are animals called arthropods, which means that they have a hard, jointed external skeleton that protects and supports their delicate insides. Insects are a special group of arthropods that have six legs and a body arranged into three parts, known as the head, the thorax, and the abdomen.

Comma butterfly

INSECT FAMILIES
Insects are divided up into different groups, called orders. All the insects in each order have similar features. For example, butterflies and moths all have two pairs of wings covered with tiny, colored scales.

A lubber grass-hopper has wings but cannot fly.

LONG JUMPERS
Grasshoppers and crickets have powerful hind legs. They move in great leaps and spring away if in danger.

DRAGON FLIGHT
The newly emerged dragon fly must wait for the network of veins to stiffen each wing before it can fly.

Vein

Antennae detect edible leaves.

A beetle's mouthparts are especially adapted to its particular diet.

CLEVER DISGUISES
Stick insects and leaf insects have some of the best camouflage of all insects. They look just like a stem or leaf of the plant on which they live.

SCARAB BEETLE
There are over three million different kinds of beetle. They use their hind wings to fly. Instead of front wings, they have hard, protective wing cases that prevent the rear wings from getting damaged.

Jointed legs

Wing cases

5

A STRONG HEAD

A close-up view of an insect's head reveals an impressive array of survival equipment. Huge eyes, containing many lenses, are quick to pick up the slightest sign of movement. The two antennae are highly sensitive, not only to touch, but also to minute traces of chemicals left in the air by other insects. The mandibles, or jaws, are different shapes to snip, slice, inject, or suck up food, depending on how the insect feeds.

LONGHORN BEETLE
The larvae of these beetles eat wood. The adult female feels a branch with her long antennae to make sure it is big enough to feed all her larvae.

SENSITIVE FEELERS
Antennae are situated at the top or tip of an insect's head. They can sample the air for smells, tastes, and vibrations.

The featherlike structure of the antennae makes them highly sensitive.

Hairy body

Antennae

WEEVIL
Weevils have a curiously long, narrow snout. Their antennae are halfway along this snout, called a rostrum, and their mouthparts are right at the end.

6

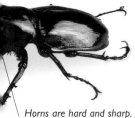

Horns are hard and sharp.

RHINOCEROS BEETLE

Male rhinoceros beetles have horns on their head and thorax. Males fight over females by locking horns and trying to overthrow each other.

JAWS OF DESTRUCTION

Locusts can swarm in such huge numbers their billions of powerful jaws can strip vast areas of land of all vegetation.

Prominent eyes can see in all directions.

This ant carries bits of leaf in its jaws back to its fungus garden.

Hard mouthparts rapidly chew up tough foliage.

ANT JAWS

Ants use their powerful jaws to carry small prey and snip up larger victims. They attack enemies by biting them, then spraying stinging acid from their rear end into the wound. The jaws are lined with serrations that are good for cutting up and gripping prey.

Serrated jaws

EYE POWER

Almost all adult insects have large compound eyes. These are made up of hundreds of units called ommatidia, which are packed tightly together. Each eye bulges out at the side of the insect's head to give it a broad field of vision. Although compound eyes have been studied by scientists, no one knows exactly what an insect can see.

HAIRY EYES

A honeybee's head and eyes are covered with hairs. These trap pollen grains as the bee forages for nectar. The bee combs the pollen off and stores it in baskets on its hind legs.

EYE DETAIL

Ommatidium

A compound eye in close-up shows each facet, or ommatidium. Every facet has its own lenses and works like a miniature eye. Although the facets look like a pattern of beads, they are actually shaped like tiny hexagons.

CATERPILLAR EYES

Unlike many other insects, caterpillars have simple eyes, which consist of layers of light-sensitive cells. These cells record light and dark, not an image. This basic information helps the caterpillar to navigate. Many adult insects have simple eyes in addition to large compound eyes.

This simple eye can detect a shadow falling over it.

LOTS OF EYES

Wraparound eyes curve around the dragonfly's face so it can see in every direction at once. The ichneumon fly on the right has two compound eyes and three simple eyes on top of its head.

Beetle eyes

NIGHT SIGHT

The eyes of night-flying insects, such as the dung beetle (top left), react to low levels of light.

Two complex eyes can see in all directions at once!

One of three simple eyes

BLUE EYES

The different colors seen on insects' eyes are caused by pigment cells surrounding each ommatidium.

The spot is the effect of light striking the eye's surface.

Long twiglike body

FURRY BODY
Pollen collects in the thick layer of fine hairs on a bumblebee's body. Pollen is rich in proteins and some will be eaten by the bee.

SHELL SUITS

Insects have no internal bones. Instead, they have an outer shell called an exoskeleton, which is connected to the insect's muscles. This tough shell is made of proteins – body chemicals that help to sustain life – and other substances, and is covered with wax to make it waterproof. As well as preventing the insect from drying out, the exoskeleton protects it from damage.

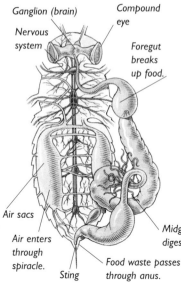

Ganglion (brain)

Nervous system

Compound eye

Foregut breaks up food.

Air sacs

Air enters through spiracle.

Sting

Midgut digests food.

Food waste passes through anus.

INSIDE AN INSECT
An insect has a simple brain and nervous system, as well as systems for digestion, respiration, excretion of wastes, and blood circulation.

An insect's leg has six segments.

HAIRY LEGS
Cockroaches hide in cracks and crevices. Spines on their legs help them grip the sides of these small openings and wriggle their way in.

Stag beetles are among the most heavily armoured beetles, thanks to their large jaws and super-hard exoskeletons.

STAG HORNS

Stag beetles fight over females and territory. The bigger beetles usually win by flipping a rival over. The loser then struggles to get back onto its feet.

These huge jaws are just for fighting; the males do not eat.

Collar protects the thorax.

LUBBER GRASSHOPPER

This grasshopper's coloured stripes warn enemies that it is poisonous. It can emit a stinking brown foam and also buzzes its wings to frighten away predators.

Wing

Long back legs

Strong legs and tough claws cling on to tree bark.

Abdomen

STING ATTACK

Many insects are armed with a painful sting. Some, such as bees, use their sting purely for self-defense, but others, such as wasps and some ants, also kill or paralyze their prey by stinging it. Venom is made by glands inside an insect's body. It is injected through a sharp, needlelike sting concealed in the tip of the insect's abdomen.

The wasp uses both her eyes and antennae to find her way around.

SYCAMORE MOTH CATERPILLAR

The tufts of fine hairs on the sycamore moth caterpillar are very brittle. They snap off easily and stick into predators. Even touching the caterpillar lightly causes an itchy red rash.

SPIDER-HUNTING WASP

This Australian female wasp uses her powerful sting to paralyze a large spider. She drags the spider to her burrow, lays a single egg on its back, and seals it inside. The wasp larva feeds on the paralyzed spider.

The sting retracts inside the abdomen when it is not in use.

WASP

Wasp venom is a cocktail of different chemicals. Some of these are actively poisonous while other ingredients help to spread the poison.

A pair of large jaws, or mandibles, carry food or nip at an enemy.

ON GUARD

Bulldog ants fiercely defend their nests. An ant grips an intruder in its serrated jaws, then swings its abdomen forward to deliver a painful sting.

REUSABLE STING

Muscles in the wasp's abdomen force the sting into a victim and then pump venom into the wound. The sting is smooth and can be retracted into the body and used again and again. A bee's sting is very different; it is armed with barbs that hook inside the wound.

Smooth sting

A slender waist gives the ant an extremely flexible body.

Unlike most ants, the bulldog ant does have a sting in its tail.

ALL TYPES OF SONG

Some insects use sounds to signal to the opposite sex. These sounds, or "songs," are frequently made by rubbing one part of the body against another, by wing-buzzing, or by foot-tapping. Each species has its own particular sequence of tunes. Singing at night is risky, since it may attract hungry bats as well as mates!

Katydids hear with "ears" on their forelegs.

This small voice box makes a very loud noise.

KATYDID
Katydids "sing" by rubbing a toothed vein on the left forewing against a hard patch on the rear of the right forewing.

CICADA
Male cicadas make throbbing sounds with two voice boxes, one on each side of the abdomen. The voice boxes vibrate and the sound is bounced off an internal amplifier.

MOSQUITO

Male and female mosquitoes make a humming sound by beating their wings. Male mosquitoes make a higher sound than females.

In a blur of movement, comblike bumps on the hind leg rub across raised veins on the wings to produce a continuous "song."

RUB-ADUB

The ribs on the locust's wing resemble a musical washboard. By rubbing the minute ridges on its hind leg back and forth across these bumpy ribs the locust "sings." Both the weather and the time of day can stimulate the locust to "sing."

The locust's "ears" are on each side of its abdomen, beneath the wings.

Mouth

Inside each hidden "ear" hole is a membrane, or eardrum.

15

Male tussur silk moth

FINDING A MATE

Like other groups of animals, male and female insects mate in order to produce eggs that hatch into a new generation. Some male insects have very large antennae that trace a female by scent. Other insects use sound or sight to find a mate. There is often rivalry between males over female insects. The males of some species take the precaution of hanging on to their mate until she has finished laying her eggs.

Female tussur silk moth

BIG LADIES

Female moths are usually bigger than males. Their bodies need to be broad to carry their bulky loads of eggs. However, males need larger antennae to scent the females.

FIREFLIES

North American fireflies are not really flies, but beetles that can make their own light. Male fireflies fly at night, flashing out signals that are seen by flightless females on the ground. Females respond by flashing back.

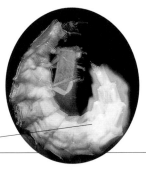

Some female fireflies copy the response of another species to lure a male that they then eat.

TUNING IN

Each delicate strand of the featherlike antennae is a separate scent detector, capable of tracking the scent of a female over a very great distance. Females often release a special scent signal, a pheromone, to help the males locate them.

A male beetle uses all six legs to hold the female during mating.

The male holds the female with a pair of special claspers at the tip of his abdomen.

TROPICAL WEEVILS

Female beetles may use scent to attract males. But many insects meet and form pairs while feeding. Large numbers of the same kinds of insect often gather around a common food source. It is the easiest way to find a mate.

LARGE RED DAMSELFLY

Just before mating, the male damselfly grips the female around the neck. The female then curves her body around so they can mate.

EGGS FIRST

Some insects lay their eggs in a pattern on twigs or under leaves to conceal them. Others spread them randomly, or scatter them on or near a food supply the larvae can eat when they hatch. A number of insects inject their eggs into the bodies of other insects. Dung beetles lay their eggs on animal droppings that they roll into a ball and bury.

FLY BAIT
Attracted by the smell of raw meat, a female greenbottle fly lays batches of white eggs on the meat surface. When the larvae hatch, they eat the flesh and grow rapidly.

The caterpillar continues to feed, while its fleshy body is incubating the eggs of the parasitic wasp.

YELLOW ICHNEUMON
Ichneumons ensure that their larvae have enough to eat by depositing them within a living caterpillar. At the same time, they inject other substances into the caterpillar to prevent it from destroying the eggs. As the parasitic wasp larvae develop, they eat their host.

OWL BUTTERFLY
These distinctive eggs are laid in groups. The color darkens when the eggs are about to hatch.

After struggling to wriggle free, the tiny caterpillar eats its eggshell.

EGG PRODUCTION
Eggs are largely made up of proteins – body chemicals that help to sustain life. Because adult butterflies only sip sugary nectar, all the necessary proteins have to be taken in while the insect is still a caterpillar.

Peacock butterfly eggs on stinging nettle leaves

Nettle stings protect the eggs from being eaten by grazing animals.

COMET OR MOON MOTH
This spectacular moth lays her eggs on a variety of plants. If one plant variety fails, only a few eggs are lost.

The female lays her eggs in batches on stems.

Each freshly laid egg is soft and sticky. As it dries, it becomes cemented firmly to the plant.

METAMORPHOSIS

The hatchlings from many insect eggs look very different from their parents. Tiny grubs called larvae hatch from the eggs of moths, butterflies, beetles, and flies. They feed and grow until it is time for the next stage in their life cycle, called pupation. A pupating insect, or pupa, may not look as though it is doing anything, but inside there is a transformation, called metamorphosis, that ends when the adult emerges.

DOT MOTH CATERPILLAR

A caterpillar's skin does not stretch, so it needs to molt as it grows. This dot moth caterpillar molts six times before it is ready to pupate underground.

SILKWORM

The common silkworm has been cultivated for over 4,000 years, and is no longer found in the wild. Each silkworm spins a bulky cocoon of silk, inside which it pupates. People unravel the cocoons and spin the silk into thread.

A silkworm is still visible inside the first layer of silk threads.

1 This postman caterpillar is a fully grown larva and is ready to pupate.

2 The caterpillar suspends itself from a small pad of silk attached to the twig above.

3 The pupa forms under the caterpillar's skin.

As the pupa develops, it wriggles to make its old skin split.

The caterpillar's skin splits, and the pupa is visible inside.

4 Continued wriggling movements make the old skin split further. Gradually the pupa struggles free of its old skin.

The old skin shrivels as it is pushed toward the twig.

5 The pupa is now free of skin, but it is still quite soft.

The pupa twists so that its tail hooks can get a grip on the silk pad.

The old skin eventually falls away, allowing the pupa to harden.

6 Inside the pupa the caterpillar's organs break down, and new limbs, muscles, and wings are formed. The irregular outline makes the pupa look like a shriveled leaf.

HONEYBEE PUPA

Protected within its wax cell, a pupating bee gradually metamorphoses into a winged adult. It is wet and bedraggled when it first emerges.

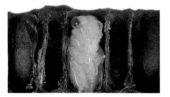

GROW UP!

Inside its pupal case, a larva changes into an adult insect. Wings, sexual organs, and sometimes even legs not present in the larva all now develop. As this transformation takes place, the outline of the winged adult may become visible. Once metamorphosis is complete, the adult emerges.

HONEYBEE

Worker honeybees feed their grubs on honey and pollen. Before pupating, each grub seals its cell by spinning a silk lid.

1 The pupal case splits around the insect's head.

2 The insect struggles to free its legs, so it can quickly push its body and wings out.

NEW BUTTERFLY

A butterfly has to struggle free from its pupal case and expand its body and wings before they harden. Otherwise it would be deformed and unable to fly.

BUFF-TIP MOTH PUPA

The bright colors of this freshly pupated moth are not often seen, because the caterpillar pupates underground.

By spreading its wings, this butterfly is camouflaged against a shady background of leaves.

WAKING BEAUTY

Newborn butterflies emerge from the lumpy pupae of the owl butterfly. The insects are very vulnerable at this stage, waiting for their wings to harden before they can fly.

Small eyespots

3 *The crumpled wings are hardly recognizable. Blood pumps into the veins, forcing the wings to expand. It takes 20 minutes for them to reach full size.*

An owl butterfly has large false eyespots on its wings to deceive predators by appearing to be an insect whose proportions match these eyes.

Antennae

BABY PRAYING MANTIS

Large numbers of tiny mantises hatch from each mass of eggs. At first the tiny hatchlings are encased in a membrane, or skin, which they later shed.

The whole cluster of hatchlings sways in unison if in danger.

SKIN CHANGE

Some groups of insects change into adults just by growing steadily. When the young insects hatch, they look rather like miniature wingless versions of the adults. This type of change is called incomplete metamorphosis. The young insects feed greedily, pausing only to shed their skins when they become too tight.

CAMEL CRICKET

Camel crickets are nocturnal insects living in walls, under bark, or in burrows. They have poor eyesight and depend on their long, sensitive antennae to locate prey.

1 As soon as the cricket's skin splits, it wriggles free as quickly as possible.

2 If it cannot free a leg, the cricket gnaws it off. The damaged limb will partially grow again.

EMPTY SKIN

A grasshopper has discarded its old skin and emerged in a new, larger skin.

GROWING UP

Three stages of growth and color change in a desert locust. The small insect needs to be well camouflaged for life on the ground because it cannot fly at this stage.

A juvenile locust is yellow and black to camouflage it in the desert.

An older locust nymph sheds its drab skin for a new black-and-white exoskeleton.

3 *The cricket frees all six legs and its two long, slender antennae. An adult camel cricket has no wings.*

EMERGING MANTIS

When it molts, a praying mantis is very vulnerable. It cannot escape from danger and has to rely on camouflage to conceal itself.

The body of a newly molted mantis expands rapidly before it hardens.

LEGGING IT

COCKROACH
The ability to run very fast is a cockroach's best method of escaping danger. They can scuttle extremely fast when disturbed, especially by light.

CATERPILLAR CRAWL
A caterpillar's eight prolegs – unjointed limbs – and two claspers have flat pads at the end. Each pad is edged with tiny hooks that help the caterpillar cling on to slippery leaves.

The true complexity of insect legs is only revealed when seen in close-up. A typical leg is made up of six segments connected to each other by joints. The large number of joints makes the legs extremely flexible. At the tip of the leg is a foot with two claws separated by a central lobe. Flies have special pads that enable them to walk upside down on smooth surfaces. The legs of other insects also show modifications that equip them for their particular lifestyles.

Six true legs

Hooks

Prolegs

These spines are used for defense.

On a twig, this spiny stick insect is well disguised.

Spiny flaps on each leg segment.

26

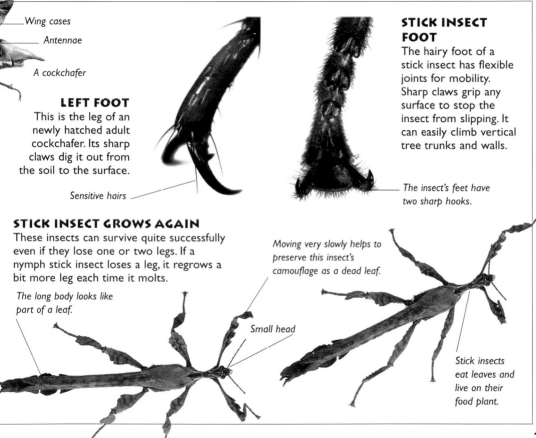

Wing cases

Antennae

A cockchafer

LEFT FOOT
This is the leg of an newly hatched adult cockchafer. Its sharp claws dig it out from the soil to the surface.

Sensitive hairs

STICK INSECT FOOT
The hairy foot of a stick insect has flexible joints for mobility. Sharp claws grip any surface to stop the insect from slipping. It can easily climb vertical tree trunks and walls.

The insect's feet have two sharp hooks.

STICK INSECT GROWS AGAIN
These insects can survive quite successfully even if they lose one or two legs. If a nymph stick insect loses a leg, it regrows a bit more leg each time it molts.

The long body looks like part of a leaf.

Moving very slowly helps to preserve this insect's camouflage as a dead leaf.

Small head

Stick insects eat leaves and live on their food plant.

SKATE OR SWIM

Many insects spend part of their lives in water and have evolved different ways of swimming and breathing. Others spend most of their lives on the surface of the water, skating over it to hunt for food and find mates. Waxy, water-repellent hairs on insects' feet prevent them from falling beneath the surface.

DIVING BEETLE

A heavy-bodied diving beetle pushes through the water, using its hind legs. Long hairs fringe its legs, which act like strong paddles. It is a fierce underwater hunter, attacking fish and tadpoles.

Thin legs for gripping on to plants.

CADDIS FLY

The larva of a caddis fly binds fragments of sticks or small stones with silk to make itself a protective case. It can crawl and swim slowly.

WATER BOATMAN

The water boatman is a predatory bug that swims upside down. It is called a water boatman because it uses its hind legs to propel itself through the water like an oarsman.

Large compound eyes for finding prey.

These underwater hunters can also fly if they need to find a new pond.

SNORKELING

Mosquito larvae poke their breathing tubes out of the water like snorkels to suck in air. They swim by wriggling their legless bodies.

These long, thin legs spread the pond skater's weight evenly over the water.

POND LOVERS

Adult pond skaters are able to mate on the surface of the water without sinking. They feed on many kinds of smaller insects, and other tiny creatures.

Pond skaters feed all summer on flying insects that fall onto the water. Surface ripples made by the struggling insects attract the skaters.

SKATING STYLE

The pond skater's splayed legs and hair-covered feet prevent it from breaking the surface tension of the water.

DRAGONFLY NYMPH

This slow-moving nymph is camouflaged by debris that clings to its body.

A MIGHTY LEAP

Most insects that jump perform their mighty leaps to escape from danger. The muscles that enable an insect to leap are attached to the inner surface of its hard exoskeleton. Some insects, such as locusts, leap into the air to rise clear of vegetation. Fleas leap to get from one animal to another.

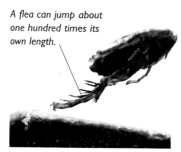

A flea can jump about one hundred times its own length.

CAT FLEA
A flea's remarkable ability to jump depends on two rubbery pads right at the base of its hind legs. These pads can be held compressed. When they are released the force triggered shoots the flea high into the air.

BUFFALO CRICKET
Most crickets have wings, but many never fly, even as adults. They rely more on jumping to get about. The buffalo cricket lives mostly on the ground, often hiding under rocks.

Long, sensitive antennae

Hind legs have big muscles.

LEAFHOPPER
This small bug leaps from leaf to leaf to escape from birds. Powerful muscles in the thorax of the hopper enable it to make sudden jumps with its hind legs.

LEAP FORWARD
A locust leaps into the air by thrusting forward on its hind legs. Its front legs are tucked under its body but will be extended to support its landing. Locusts fly when they need to move farther afield.

The long, narrow front wings protect the wide hind wings.

Compound eye

Earth-colored abdomen

The short-legged springtail lives on the surface of stagnant pools.

GRASSHOPPER
Black and brown grasshoppers are camouflaged for life on the ground, especially in desert regions. They jump between feeding sites, moving speedily without using their wings.

WATER TRICKS
Beneath the abdomen of the short-legged springtail is a forked-spring mechanism that can propel the insect up into the air to escape any predator.

PRAYING MANTIS
Male mantises have wings, but the females of some kinds are wingless and wait patiently for the males to find them. Although a flying mantis looks ungainly on the wing, it is surprisingly fast and direct in flight.

The front wings give lift and balance.

Hind wings provide the power for flight.

The ability to fly gives insects many advantages over other creatures. Flight enables insects to escape from their enemies and to look for new sources of food. Insects may fly a long way to find a mate, and some migrate thousands of miles to spend the winter in warmer places.

Getting ready for take off, the two wing cases of the ladybug part slightly.

HIDDEN WINGS
The front or forewings of beetles have evolved into hard, protective wing cases called elytra. Beetles only use their hind wings for flying. At rest a ladybug's wings are hidden.

CRANE FLY

Crane flies have long, narrow wings and flutter about weakly. They usually fly at dusk to avoid predators.

Instead of hind wings, flies have a pair of knobbed structures called halteres. These rotate in flight, helping the insect to balance.

LIFT OFF

Ladybugs fly in search of food, a mate, or to seek a place to lay eggs. A few fly to hibernate in cracks and crevices.

4 *Outstretched legs balance the insect on its clumsy flight..*

The bold pattern of black spots warns birds that ladybugs taste disgusting.

Segmented abdomen

2 *The wing cases spread and pivot forward on hinges.*

3 *The filmy hind wings unfold. The ladybug is ready for take off. Its large, transparent wings help it to fly surprisingly fast.*

IN FLIGHT

Dragonflies' wing-beats are slow; just 30–50 per second.

The earliest known fossils of winged insects are about 300 million years old. These were dragonflies, very similar to species living today. Insects have evolved over time, and they now have a fantastic variety of wing shapes and sizes. The shape of the wing determines how an insect flies. Some fly in straight lines while others flutter from side to side.

DRAGON FLIGHT

The way a dragonfly flies is quite amazing. It can beat both pairs of wings in unison to fly fast. It can also beat its fore and hind wings independently. This enables it to take off in reverse, or stop dead in midflight and hover.

PERICOPID MOTH

The fore and hind wings of all moths are linked together so that they flap in unison. Muscles in an insect's thorax move the wings up and down.

1 As the wings flap, they twist slightly, so that the wing tips move through a figure-eight pattern.

2 This figure-eight motion makes air flow downward and backward, lifting the insect forward.

3 *The moth flaps its wings above its back, then brings them down to create an area of air turbulence beneath it.*

WING SCALES
The surface of a butterfly or moth wing is hairy. Each microscopic hair is flattened and as small as a particle of dust. Color and patterns provide camouflage.

Bright wing colors frighten predators.

FLIGHT PATHS
A dragonfly relies on fast, level flight to catch its prey and escape from danger. Butterflies zigzag from side to side to confuse pursuing predators.

Dragonfly

Butterfly

4 *The downward flap is the power stroke, lifting the moth forward as turbulent air flows over the wings.*

FEEDING TIME

Plant-sucking aphid

Ladybug feasting

LADYBUG

Both ladybug beetles and their larvae are gardeners' friends. They feed greedily on plant-damaging aphids, crawling up stems and eating them one after the other.

Insects may be small, but the effects of large numbers of them munching away can be devastating. They can strip the leaves and fruit from trees and fields; some insects can reduce buildings to dust. However, there are adult insects that do not feed at all. Others are beneficial to humans: plant-sucking aphids are eaten by ladybug larvae, and dung and carrion beetles clean up animal droppings and remains, like miniature garbage collectors.

Segmented body

MEALWORM BEETLE LARVAE

Not a fussy eater, this larva may be found feeding on debris in old birds' nests as well as in stored cereal products. Lots of them can devour the contents of a sack of flour or a grain bin.

This larva has micro-organisms in its gut that help it digest plant cellulose, its main food source.

STAG BEETLE GRUB
A stag beetle grub has to feed on wood for three years before it is ready to pupate. It grows slowly because wood is very low in nutrients.

Huge jaws for sawing wood.

WELL CHEWED
A caterpillar eats continually, to store enough protein for laying eggs when it is a moth. It works its jaws, called mandibles, from side to side as it chews through leaves and other edible plant matter. With a good food supply caterpillars can grow at a phenomenal rate.

DESERT STORM
A large swarm of locusts containing billions of hungry insects can blot out the sun like a cloud. Locusts eat every leaf in sight. As soon as they have stripped the vegetation in one place, they fly off to find food somewhere else.

WASP FOOD
In summer, wasps hunt for other insects, which they snip up and carry back to their nest. They chew these bits of insect to a pulp, and then feed the pulp to the wasp grubs.

Warning colors

A wasp enjoys the sweet juice from an autumn apple.

HANDS UP!

Insects use their six legs for more than just moving over the ground. Some insects have one or more pairs of highly specialized legs, modified to catch and hold their prey ready for eating. Others have legs and feet designed to dig for food. Some insects' legs are used like hands, to carry food back to the nest.

Hairy legs

Strong jaws

Antennae

Grasping claws

DIVING BEETLE

The diving beetle is a fierce predator. It uses its forelegs to grab and hold its prey. It can chase and grab underwater victims because it carries an air supply under its wings.

Tail resembles a sting.

Prolegs are muscular extensions of the body wall. They support the bulky body of the caterpillar.

PRIVET HAWK MOTH CATERPILLAR

Four pairs of prolegs and one pair of claspers grip the leaves of a caterpillar's food plant. Six true legs help with walking and also guide leaves into the caterpillar's jaws.

Six true legs

LEAF EATERS
A locust feeds, holding on to each side of a blade of grass and leaning forward to chew.

QUICK BITE
A mantis uses speed and rows of spines on its front legs to grab a snack out of the air.

A mantis starts to feast on a fly it has grabbed for dinner.

The forelegs are particularly large and have sharp claws to help it dig.

CLEAN AND TIDY
Honeybees comb pollen from their bodies and press it into hair-fringed "baskets" on their hind legs to carry it back to the hive.

MOLE CRICKET
The mole cricket feeds on underground roots. All six of its legs are especially adapted for burrowing,

The tip of the proboscis dips into each flower to find nectar.

DRINKING TIME

Flowers produce sweet, sugary nectar to attract insects and other animals. While they are foraging for nectar, these creatures unwittingly pollinate the plant. As a food, nectar is high in energy-giving carbohydrates but very low in bodybuilding proteins, so insects that feed their young on nectar also collect some high-protein pollen for their larvae to eat. Flowers, rich in nectar, use color and scent to attract insect pollinators.

CLOUDED YELLOW BUTTERFLY
A butterfly has a long, slender proboscis, rather like a straw, with which it sucks up nectar. After feeding, the proboscis rolls up in a neat coil.

BUMBLEBEE
This short-tongued bumblebee can only reach nectar in flat flowers. To reach nectar in long-tubed flowers, the bee bites holes in the flower tube close enough to reach the nectar.

HUMMINGBIRD HAWKMOTH

The hummingbird hawkmoth is active in the daytime. It hovers without settling, using its extremely long proboscis to probe deep into flowers such as honeysuckle.

The proboscis, a drinking tube, looks like the insect's nose.

FURRY FACE

The butterfly's small face is covered with hairs. Its large eyes have all-around vision. Its proboscis is neatly coiled away.

This hoverfly is foraging among the broad petals of a meadow cranesbill flower.

OWL BUTTERFLY

Butterflies do not only take food from flowers. The sweet, fermenting sap of rotting fruit also attracts them. Some butterflies even sip from decaying flesh or puddles of urine.

This butterfly is feeding on the sugary fruit juice.

HOVERFLY

Newly emerged male hoverflies and all females feed on pollen. Females need the protein it provides for making eggs. Males switch to sipping nectar when they start to seek females for mating.

These flies have taste receptors on their feet, so they can tell when they land on something edible. Flies will eat anything they can digest.

Wings

Traveling between a garbage can to uncovered food in a kitchen is how a fly spreads germs.

SUCKING UP

Sucking up liquid food is easy for an insect. It draws the fluid up through a tubular arrangement of mouthparts in much the same way as a person drinks through a straw. To reach juicy saps, plant-sucking insects have sharp mouthparts that cut into plant stems. Flies feed on a variety of solid foods. They dribble out saliva that contains enzymes to digest and liquefy the food, and then suck it up.

SHIELDBUG
Bugs that feed on the sap of shrubs or trees have needle-sharp mouthparts that penetrate tough foliage and stems. The mouthparts fold away when not in use.

A drop of sweet nectar hangs from the proboscis of this parasitic fly.

Ants look after groups of scale bugs. They collect up the honeydew produced by the bugs.

Scale bug

SUCKING UP
A spongy, grooved pad drips saliva onto food to break it down before a fly can suck up the liquefied food through its proboscis, a long mouthpart similar to a drinking straw.

Proboscis

Aphid

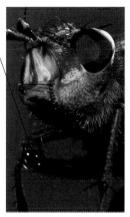

SCALE BUG
These tiny, plant-sucking bugs feed on plant stems. Each nymph secretes a waxy shell, or scale, over itself. Protected beneath this scale, it feeds and matures, and lays its eggs before dying.

Winged male scale bugs are rare. Wingless females can reproduce without mating.

APHID
Aphids are soft-bodied bugs. Their mouthparts are so small and weak that they only take sap from the juicy tips and growing points of fresh plants. They multiply so rapidly they are a common garden pest.

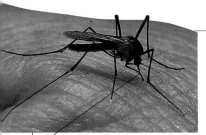

A mosquito bite is usually painless. The painful reaction of an itchy swelling lump is due to an allergic response to the mosquito's saliva.

BLOOD SUCKERS

Some insects feed on blood, since it is rich in protein and easy to swallow. These insects have such sharp, stabbing mouthparts they often pierce the skin of their victims without being noticed. Blood-sucking insects also have substances called anticoagulants in their saliva, to keep the blood runny and prevent it from clotting. Many of these insects carry diseases that they pass on with each bite.

MOSQUITO

A female mosquito pierces an animal's skin to obtain a meal of blood before producing her eggs. As her mouthparts penetrate a tiny blood vessel, saliva pours into the puncture to stop the blood clotting. Saliva may contain organisms that cause malaria.

The robber fly imprisons its prey in a deadly clasp.

Clawed feet

DEADLY KILLER

The robber fly is a fierce predator. It catches prey in flight and carries it to a perch. The fly injects a digestive saliva into its victim. This liquifies the victim's internal organs, which the fly can then suck up.

Tsetse fly prefers to bite a thin patch of skin.

Before feeding, a tsetse fly has a slim body.

FULL FLY

A tsetse fly sucks human or animal blood through its mouth tube and stores it in its body cavity. In Africa the tsetse fly is a known carrier of several infections of the blood including Chagas' disease and sleeping sickness.

Swollen and red with blood, this tsetse fly is still sucking.

A female cleg fly

CLEG FLY

Female clegs feed on blood. This provides them with the proteins they need to produce eggs. Males feed on nectar.

BLUE TIT FLEA

Fleas multiply in bird's nests all summer, feeding on the blood of nestlings and brooding parents. They survive the winter among the nest debris. Blue tits tend to return to the same nest each year, but if there are too many fleas in the nest, they will abandon it.

Fleas have deep, flat bodies.

COLONIAL LIVING

Huge numbers of termites, ants, bees, and wasps often live together in colonies. The organization of these colonies is complex, since every insect has a particular role. Workers build the nest, hunt for food, and clean the colony. Some colonies are protected by soldier insects that stand guard and repel intruders. A single queen insect usually lays all the eggs. But some really large ant nests have more than one egg-laying queen.

WOOD ANTS

Wood ants have strong jaws. Any insect or invertebrate that strays too close to a wood ant's foraging area is at risk. A large number of ants will overpower an intruder and drag it back to their nest.

BLACK GARDEN ANT

The queen lays all the eggs which are looked after, along with the larvae, by the workers. The workers keep the eggs free from fungus and feed the larvae on sugars and chewed insect material.

The white pupae are put in warm spots in the soil or under a stone.

TERMITE

Worker termites tunnel into wood to extend their colony. The wood is also used to feed their grubs. Soldier termites guard the nest.

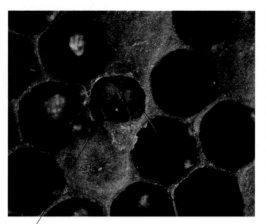

Each cell contains a single bee grub.

BEE'S WAX

In their wax cells bee grubs, larvae, are fed by worker bees. When ready to pupate they spin a door of silk to seal the cell. Later they emerge and spend a short time in the hive before flying off to collect nectar as worker bees. Their cells are cleaned and reused.

HONEYBEE BABIES

The queen lays up to 1,000 eggs every day. Most are fertilized eggs that hatch into female bees. A few are laid in special queen comb-cells and fed on royal jelly and honey. They will become new queens. The rest are fed honey and become workers. Unfertilized eggs become male bees and mate with the queens.

A newly hatched hive bee emerges from its cell.

The bee dances, in a sequence of moves, to show the workers the route to the honey.

DANCE TALK

Returning workers dance to show other bees where to find food. They step out patterns; circles and figure eights. The bee may also wiggle its abdomen. Wing-buzzing, speed, and the length of the dance also have special meanings.

HOUSE BUILDING

Insect builders use their mandibles to construct nests in which their young larvae develop. Social bees, ants, wasps, and termites build gigantic nests that contain thousands or even millions of insects. These huge nests are built by the cooperative effort of worker insects. The much smaller nests of solitary bees and wasps are just as finely made.

TERMITE MOUND
This mound of rock-hard mud and termite droppings encloses an intricate termite city of air-cooled passageways, fungus farms, and nursery chambers full of larvae. The mound acts as a chimney, drawing air out of the mound to cool the passageways below.

WEAVER ANT
To make their nest, a row of worker weaver ants pulls two leaf edges close together. Other workers hold ant larvae in their mandibles, stimulating them to produce silk, which is used to weave the leaf edges together. Only the larvae are able to produce the silk needed for nest building.

MUD-DAUBER WASP
A solitary mud-dauber wasp makes a small, round clay cell. She places a paralyzed insect or spider inside, as food for the grub that will hatch from her single egg.

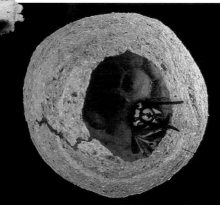

ROYAL BUILDER
A queen wasp chews fragments of wood into a papery pulp to make a few hexagonal cells ready to receive her first eggs. Around them, using her mouthparts, she molds a hanging sphere. Workers complete the nest.

This nest is beautifully spherical.

Ants carrying pieces of leaf cannot defend themselves from parasitic flies.

Only the larger worker ants have strong enough jaws to cut and carry the huge pieces of leaf.

LEAF CUTTER ANTS
The largest worker ants snip leaves into pieces to carry to their nest. Other workers then chew the leaves to a pulp, mix it with their droppings, and use the resulting paste to grow a type of fungus, on which the colony depends for food.

HIDDEN FROM VIEW

The caterpillar looks just like a short, knobly twig.

GARDEN CARPET MOTH CATERPILLAR

This caterpillar adopts a twiglike posture to avoid being seen. It stays quite still, because any movement would immediately betray its presence to a passing bird.

One way for an insect to avoid being eaten is to blend perfectly into the background, so that a predator simply cannot see it. Insects that use camouflage to survive usually stay quite still during the day and only become active after dark, when they feed. Both shape and color contribute to camouflage, which can be so effective that the insect is virtually invisible within its normal surroundings.

CASE OR BAG MOTH CATERPILLAR

The larvae of this moth spin cases of silk around themselves. Tiny bits of plant debris or other small particles stick to the outside and camouflage the silk bag. Some of the adult female moths are wingless, and spend their whole lives inside their bag.

The caterpillar pokes its head through a front opening.

Leaves are used for camouflage.

LEAF COVER

This small area of bark and dead leaves hides four woodland moths.

Antennae

1
2
3
4

Thin brown body

RED UNDERWING

Long antennae

This night-flying moth rests during the day. Once it has settled on the rough bark of a tree, the mottled gray pattern on its fore wings provides perfect camouflage.

STICK INSECT

With their long legs and thin bodies, stick insects have perfected the art of looking like a slender twig or blade of grass. They are invisible until they move slowly to another branch.

LEAF INSECT

Leaf insects remain undetected because they resemble the leaves of their food plants. They even have the pattern of veins, tears, and other marks characteristic of green leaves.

The front of this leaf insect resembles a chewed leaf.

COPY CATS

By adopting various shapes or patterns, some insects disguise themselves as something quite different from what they really are. This form of imitation is called mimicry. Insects either mimic poisonous or distasteful species, such as wasps or ants, or they imitate unappetizing items, such as animal droppings. Mimicry has clear advantages. A predator will avoid the mimics as much as it avoids the insects that they successfully copy.

False-eye spot

FALSE EYES
Eyes are a focal point for birds and mammals. If eyes are large and alarming, the message is that the animal is big and dangerous. Many insects trick predators by sporting huge false eyespots on their bodies or wings.

As the caterpillar gets bigger, it changes its appearance to blend in better with its background.

CITRUS SWALLOWTAIL CATERPILLAR
The young caterpillars of swallowtail butterflies are brown, and shiny, and blotched with white to mimic fresh bird droppings on a leaf.

Dark face

DEAD CENTER

The orchid mantis sways gently from side to side with the petals, disguised as the center of a fading flower. It crouches, ready to pounce on any nectar-seeking insect that approaches.

ORCHID MANTIS

The translucent flaps on this mantis's legs look just like petals. Brown blotching and veining on its back and wings make it resemble a fading orchid blossom.

WASP MIMIC

At first glance, this hoverfly is easily mistaken for a wasp. It is about the same size and shape, and has the warning yellow and black stripes of the venomous wasp. But this harmless fly has no sting.

The wasp has regular eyes and short antennae.

A wasp has two pairs of narrow wings.

The hoverfly has large eyes and short antennae.

Similar colouring

A hoverfly has a pair of large wings.

Harlequin bug

INDEX

Swallowtail butterfly

*Nepheronia
butterfly*

Dune beetle

Chafer beetle